Icebr...

Written by Jo Windsor

PIERRE RADISSON

CONTENTS

Harcourt Achieve

Rigby · Saxon · Steck-Vaughn

www.HarcourtAchieve.com
1.800.531.5015

Why We Have Icebreakers

In winter, cold temperatures freeze the water. The ice is very thick. No ships can come and go through the ice. When this happens, a ship called an icebreaker is used to break up the ice.

Icebreakers are very big ships specially made for breaking ice. They have been used for a long time. Icebreakers help keep the seas cleared of ice so ships can move from place to place. They make sure that ships can go through the frozen water all winter long.

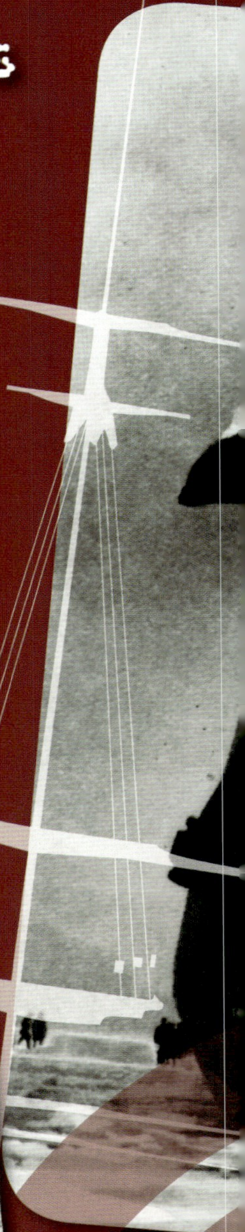

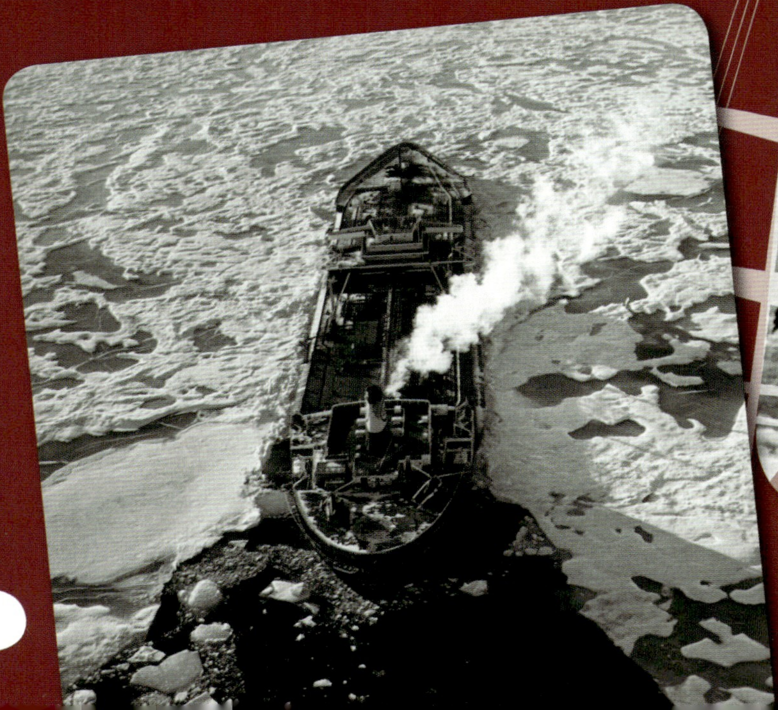

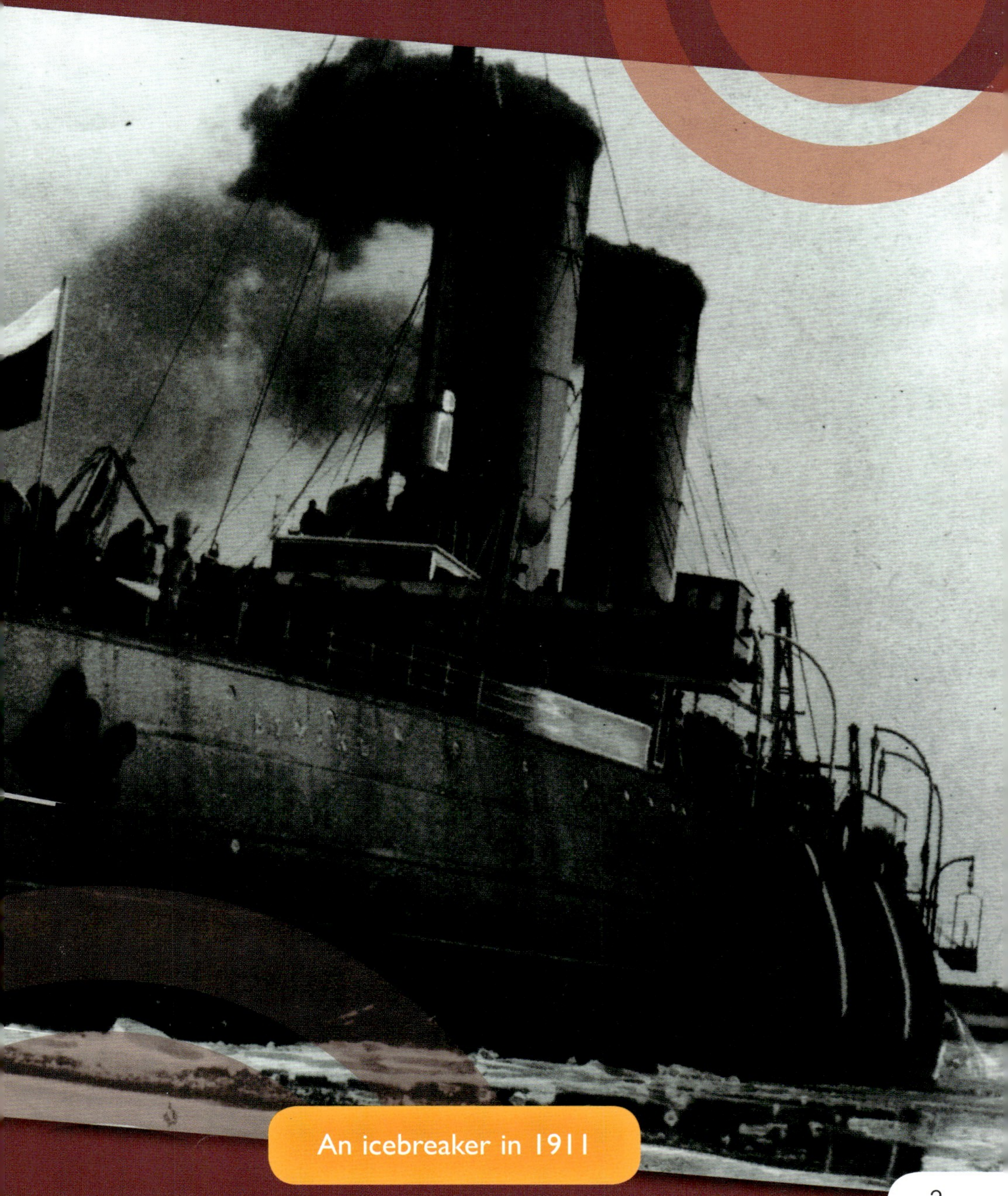

An icebreaker in 1911

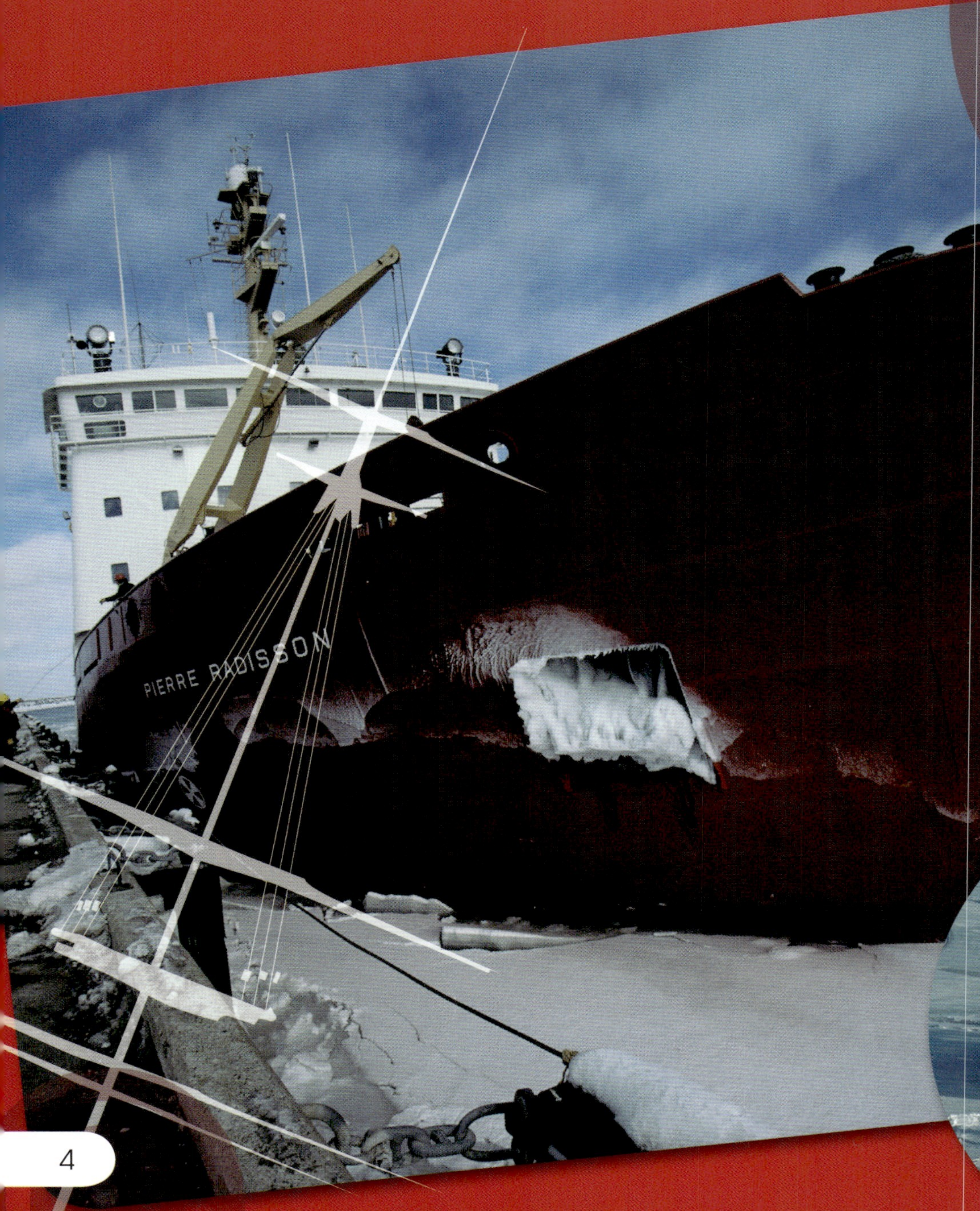
PIERRE RADISSON

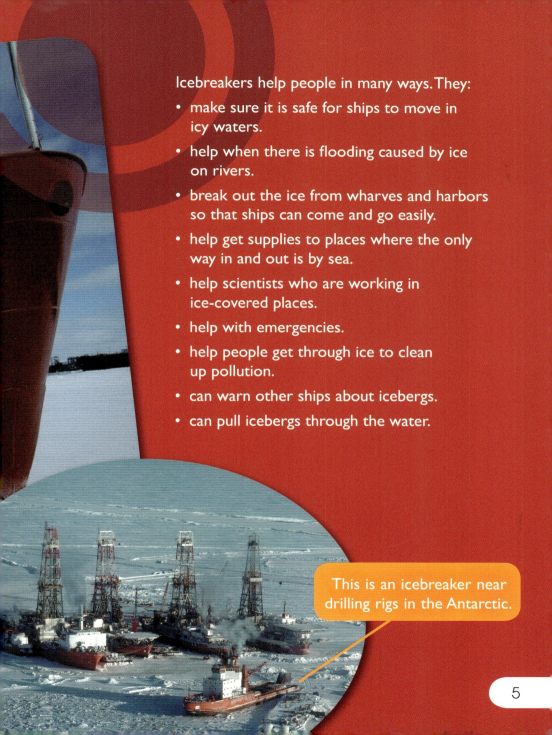

Icebreakers help people in many ways. They:

- make sure it is safe for ships to move in icy waters.
- help when there is flooding caused by ice on rivers.
- break out the ice from wharves and harbors so that ships can come and go easily.
- help get supplies to places where the only way in and out is by sea.
- help scientists who are working in ice-covered places.
- help with emergencies.
- help people get through ice to clean up pollution.
- can warn other ships about icebergs.
- can pull icebergs through the water.

This is an icebreaker near drilling rigs in the Antarctic.

What Icebreakers Look Like

Icebreakers are built in a special shape. They are much wider than other ships. Some icebreakers can be 100 feet wide. This helps the ship clear a path through the ice that is wide enough for other ships to go through.

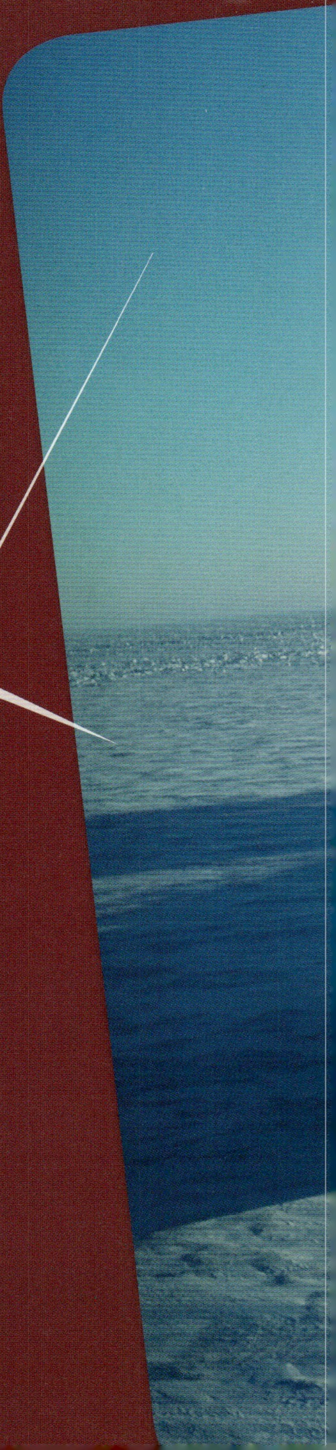

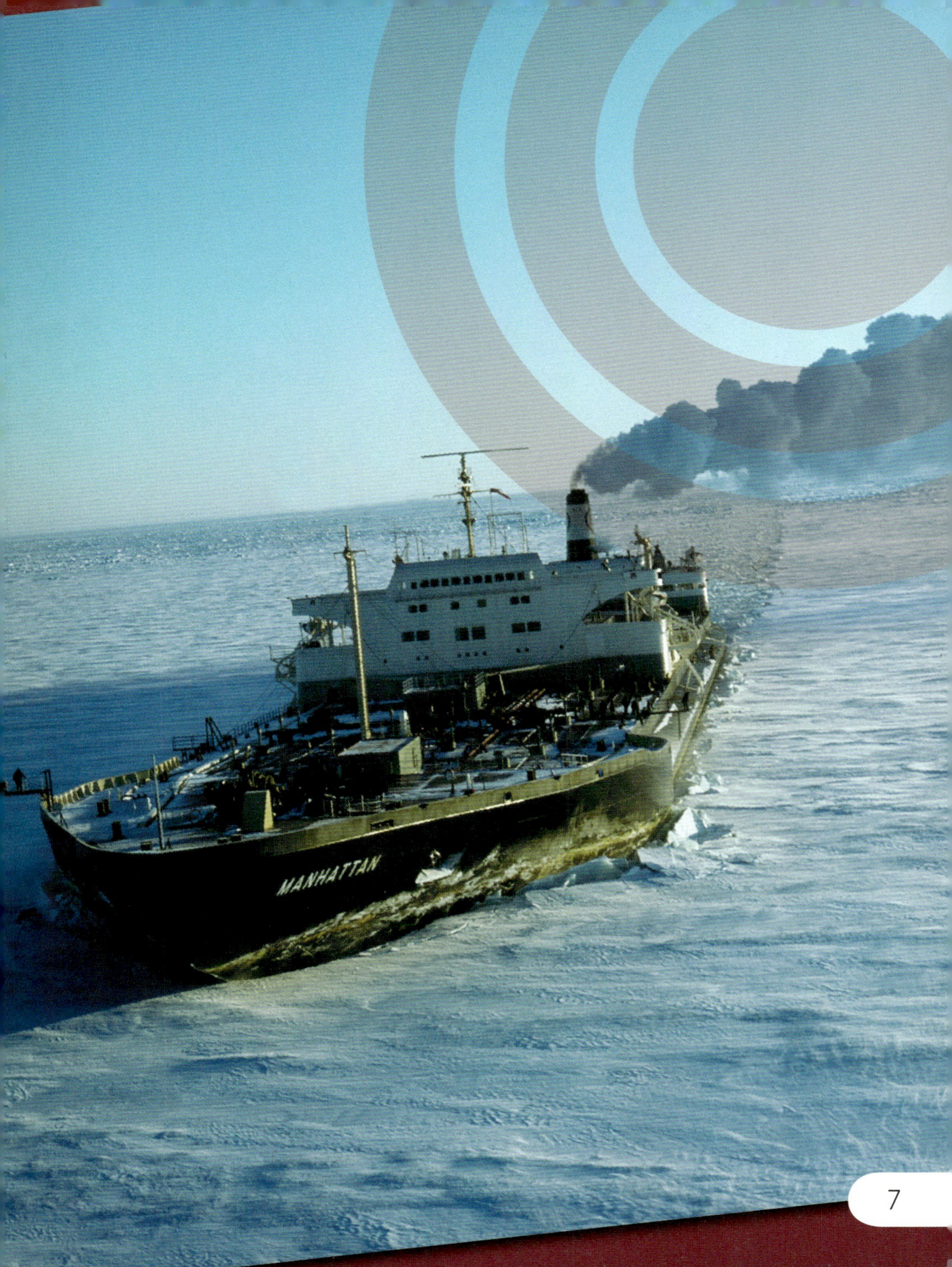
MANHATTAN

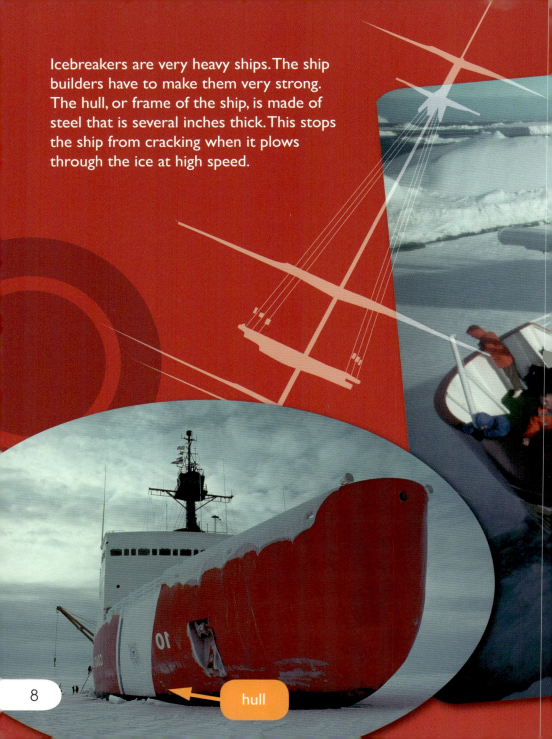

Icebreakers are very heavy ships. The ship builders have to make them very strong. The hull, or frame of the ship, is made of steel that is several inches thick. This stops the ship from cracking when it plows through the ice at high speed.

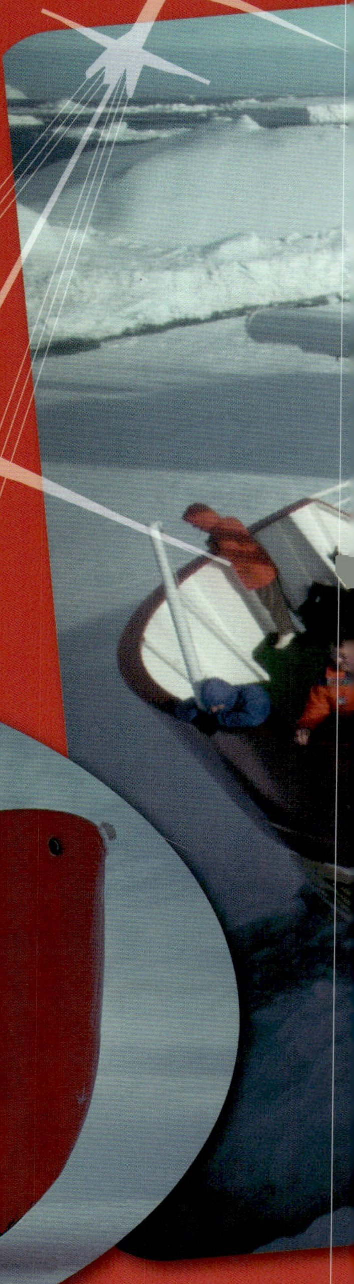

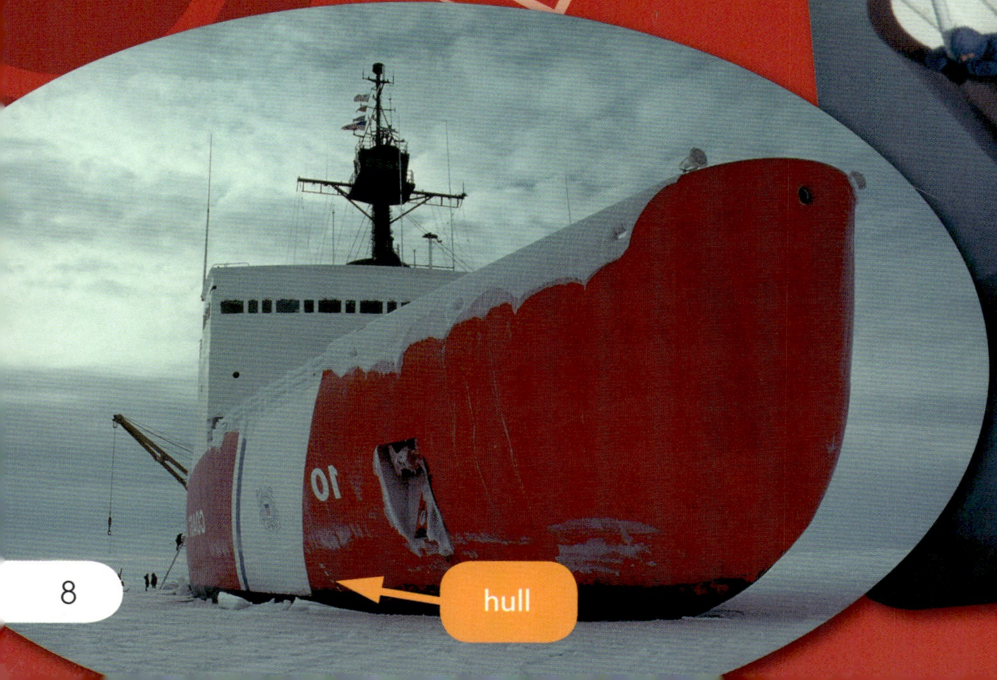
hull

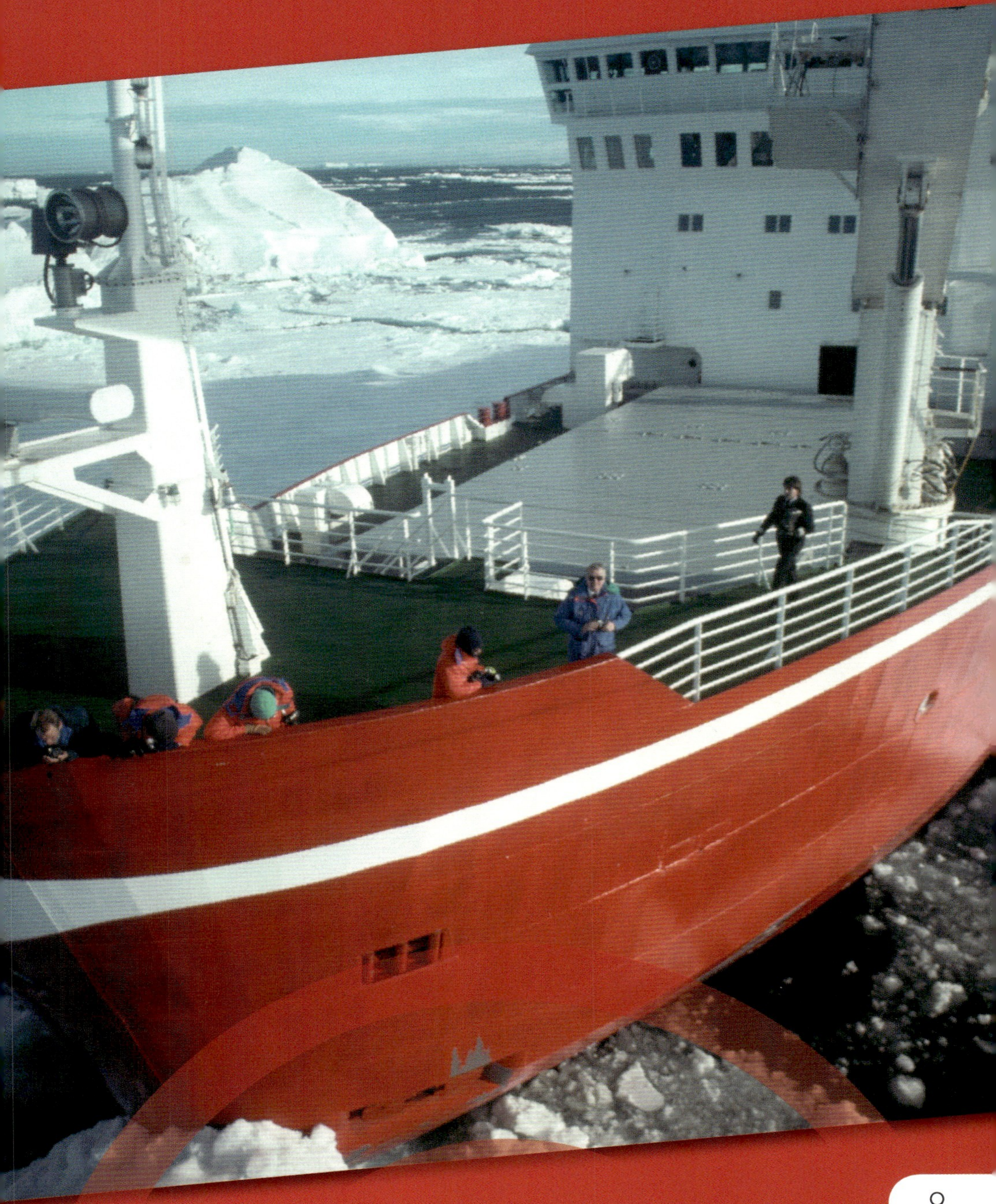

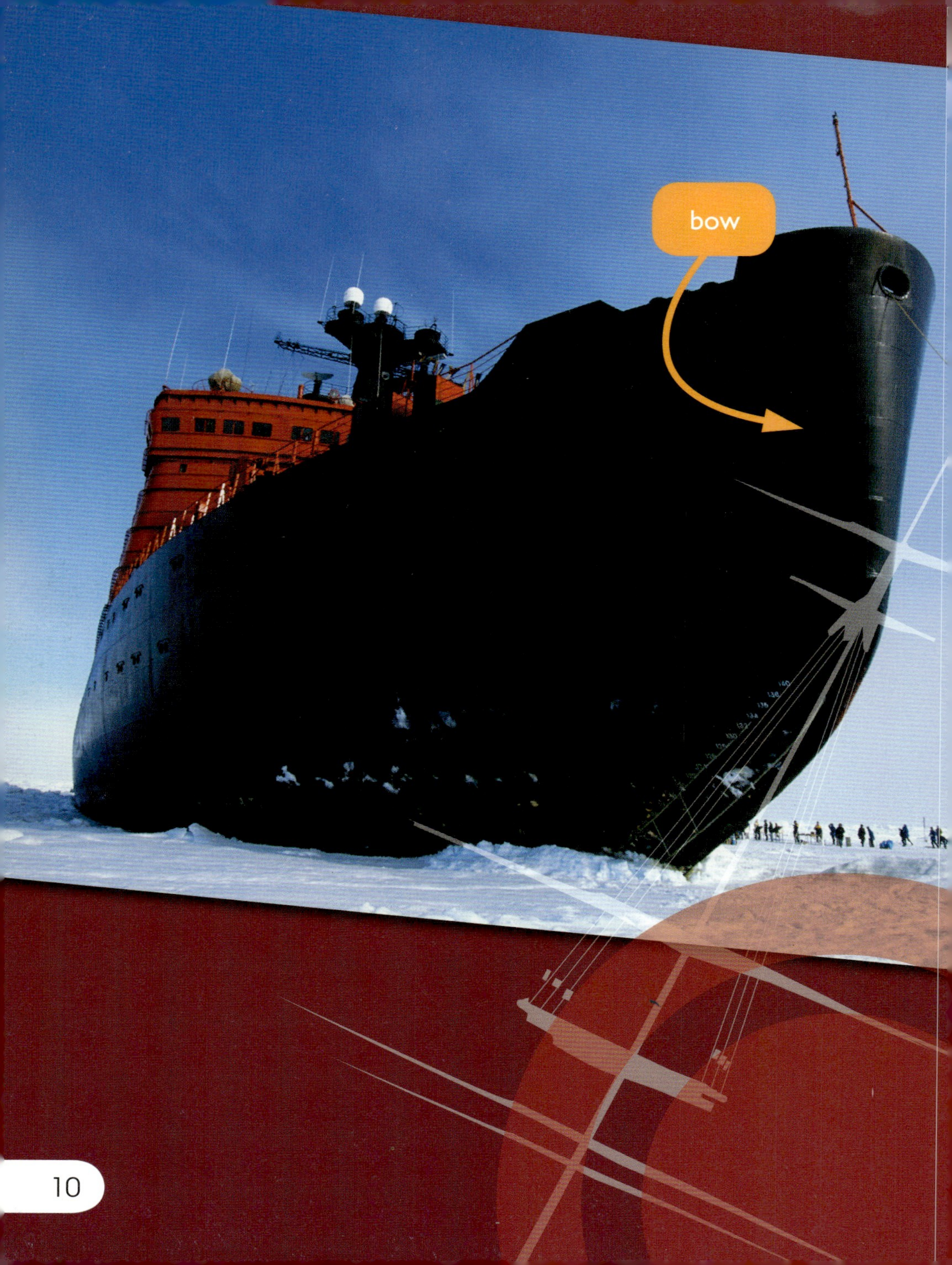
bow

The front of the ship is called the bow. The hull under the bow is shaped like a knife. This helps the icebreaker cut through the ice.

The back of the ship is called the stern. Huge propellers are under the stern. These propellers push the ship forward. Icebreakers have powerful engines that turn the huge propellers. They push the ship through the ice. Sometimes the ice can be more than seven feet thick.

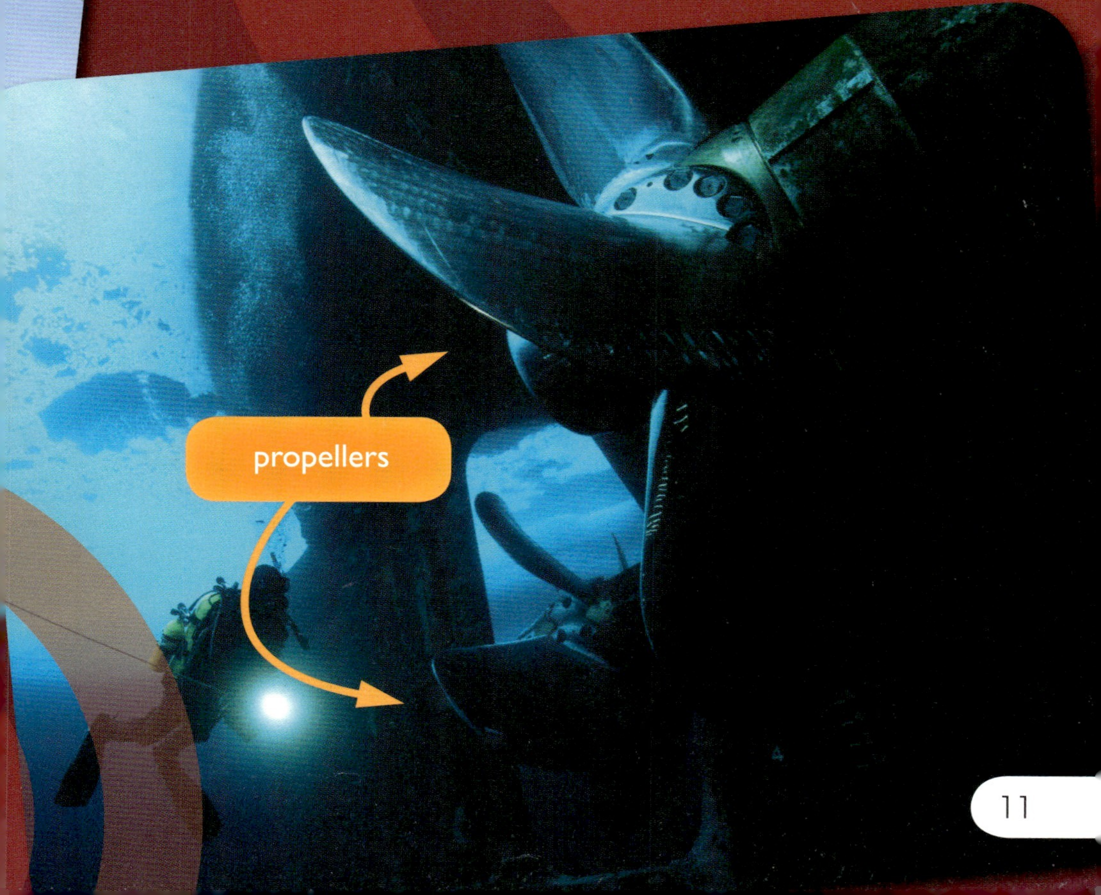
propellers

What Icebreakers Do

1. Powerful engines push the icebreaker forward. The bow slides the ship up on the ice. This puts a lot of weight on the ice.

2. The icebreaker keeps moving forward and up onto the ice.

3. The weight of the icebreaker causes the ice to break up in big chunks.

4. The broken ice is pushed out of the way as the icebreaker moves forward through the water.

This happens again and again, as the icebreaker clears a way through the ice.

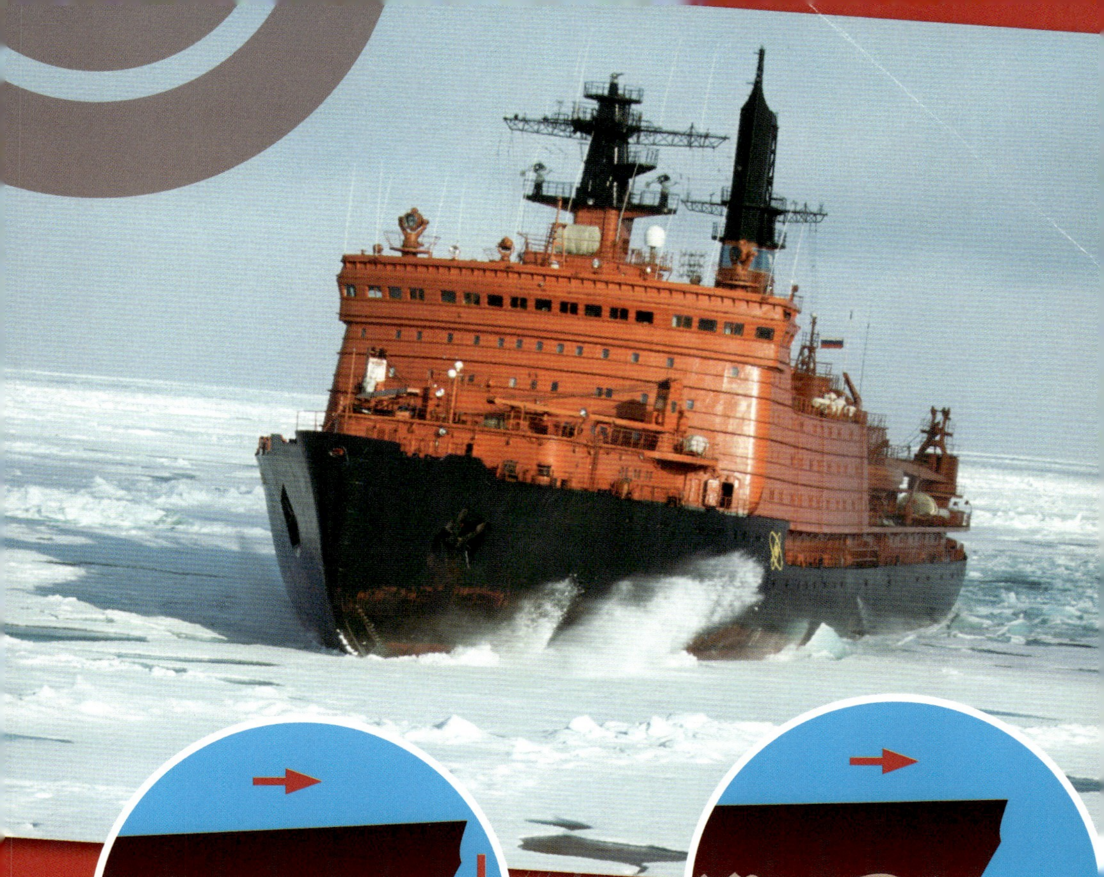

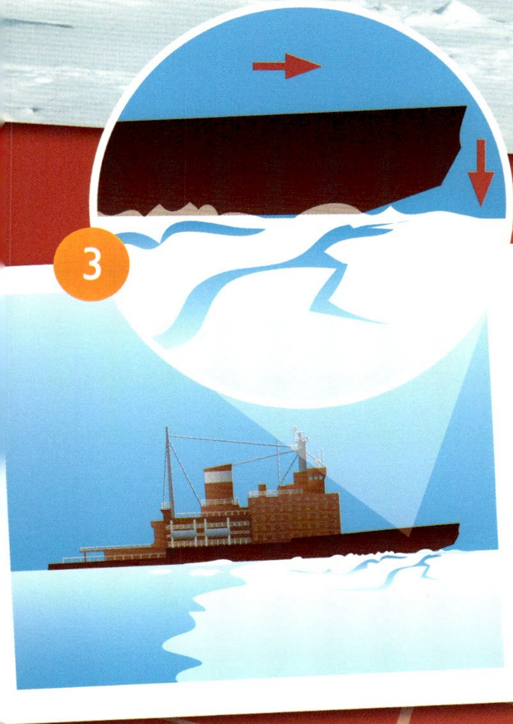
3

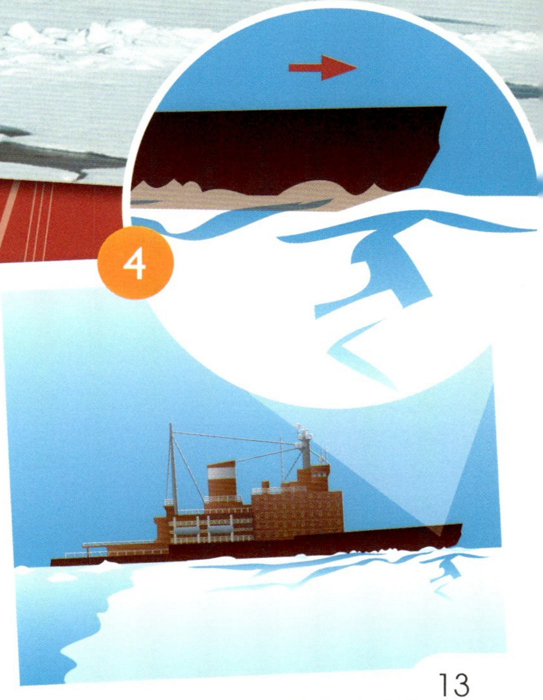
4

The Crew of an Icebreaker

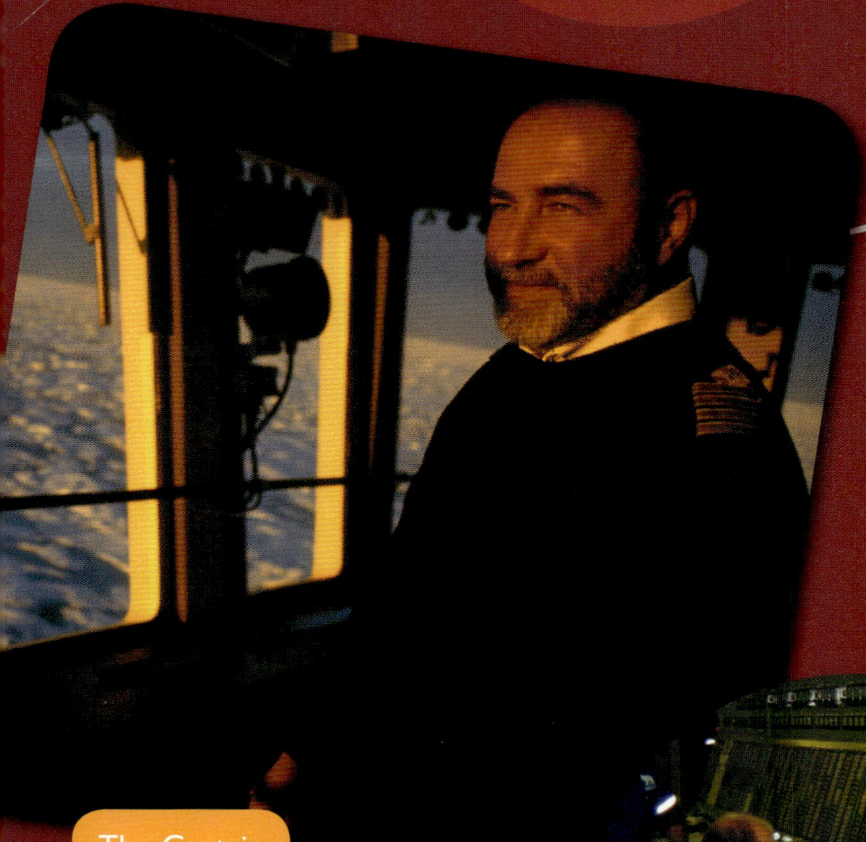

The Captain

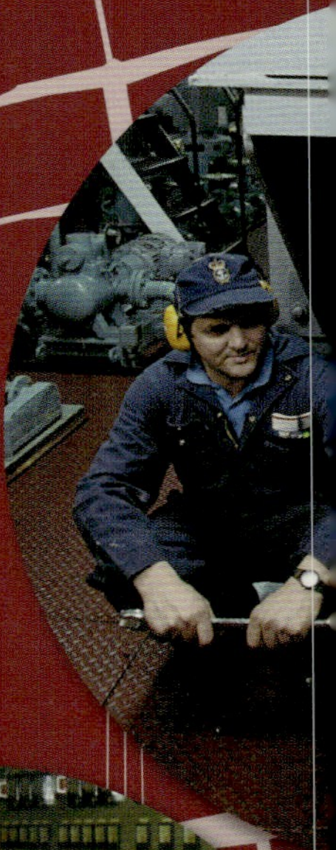

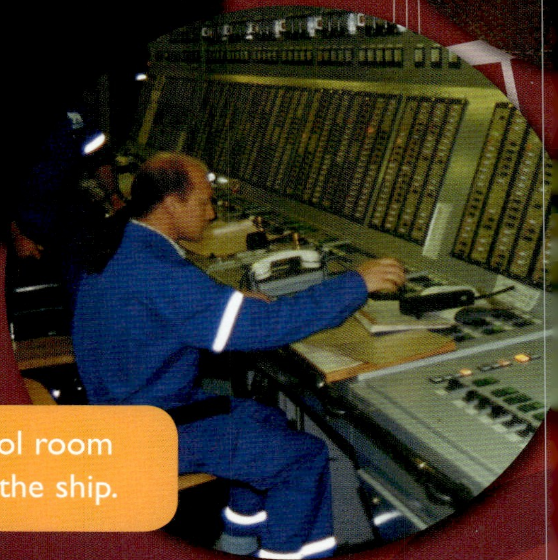

The crew in the control room control everything on the ship.

There may be more than 100 crew members aboard an icebreaker. The captain controls the icebreaker from the bridge at the top of the ship. The crew are well trained for working in very difficult and dangerous conditions.

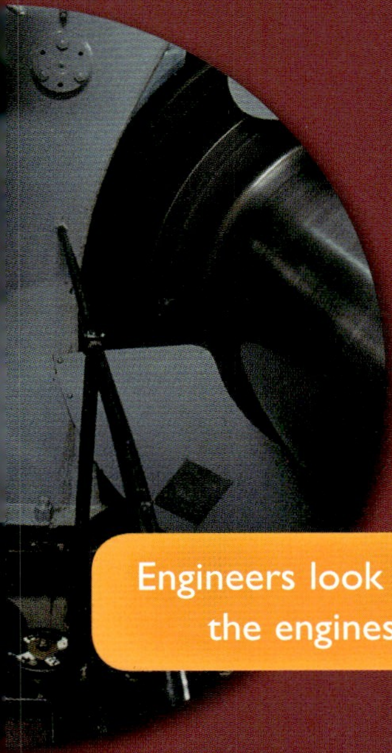

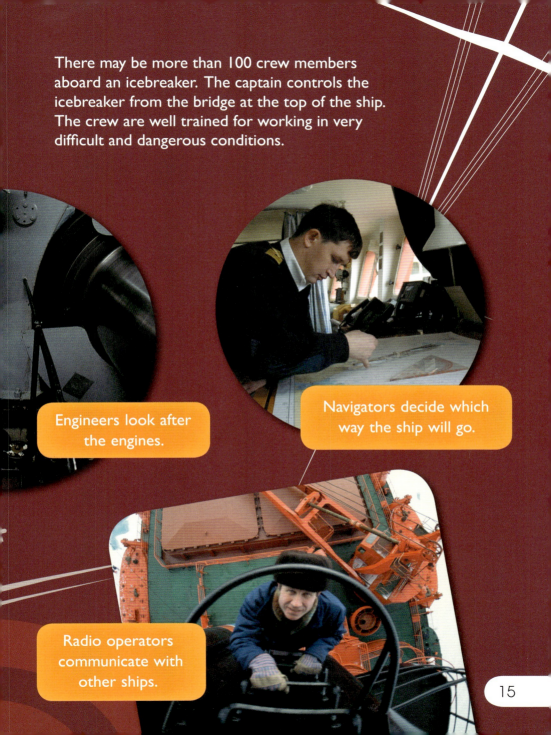

Engineers look after the engines.

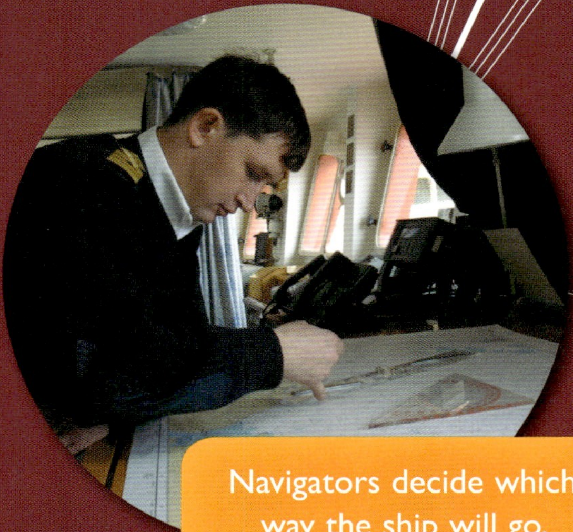

Navigators decide which way the ship will go.

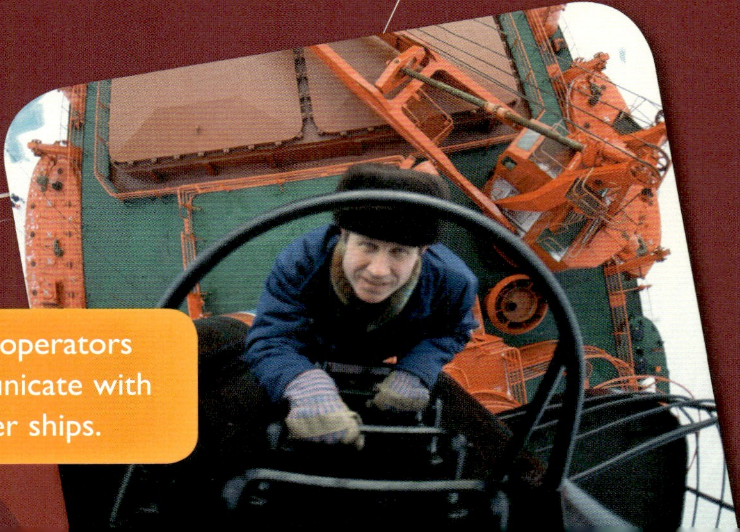

Radio operators communicate with other ships.

The crew need to be ready to take an icebreaker where normal ships cannot go.

Ice and icebergs are a problem for normal ships, but not for icebreakers. They can easily break up sheets of ice with their strong hulls, their powerful engines, and their heavy weight.

Icebreakers and their crews help other ships keep sailing. They make a way in and out of places that would otherwise be cut off by the ice.

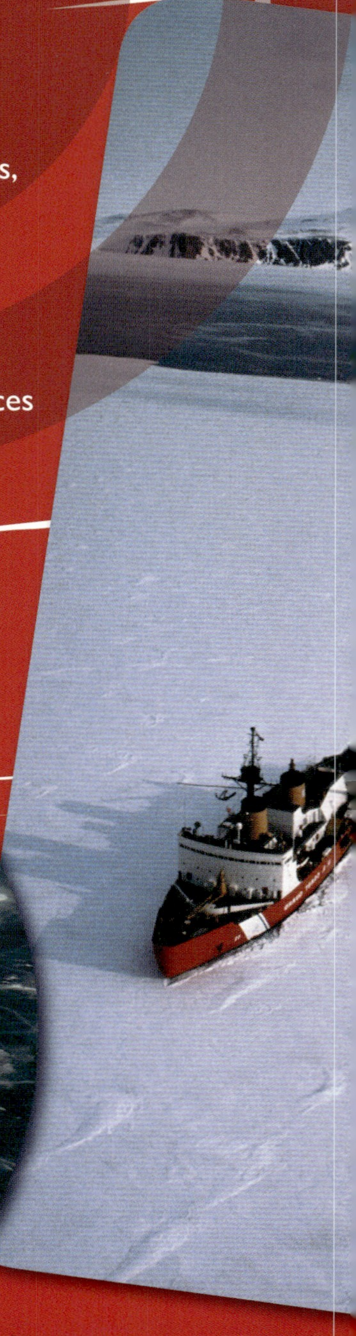

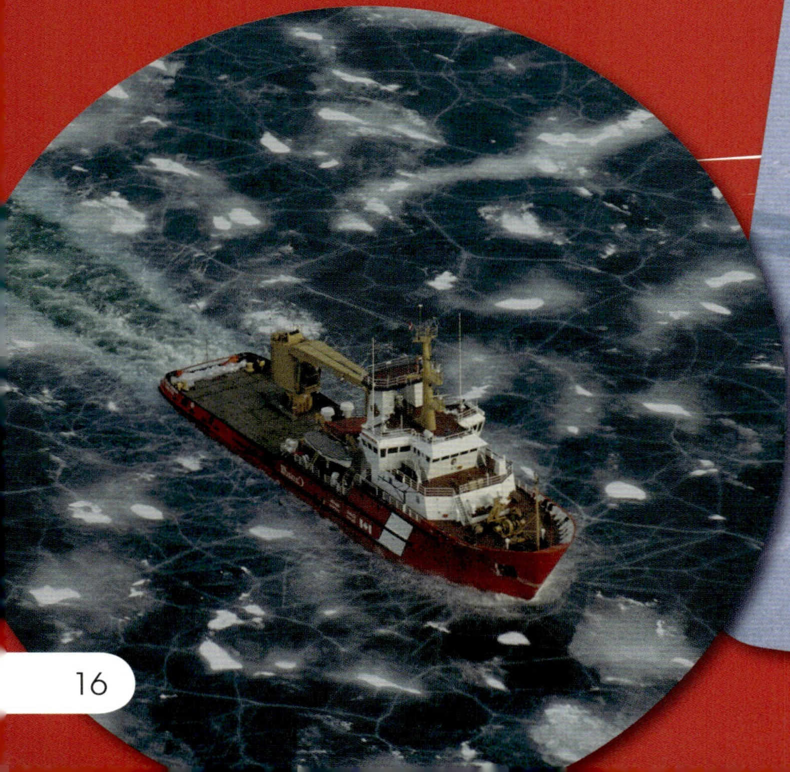

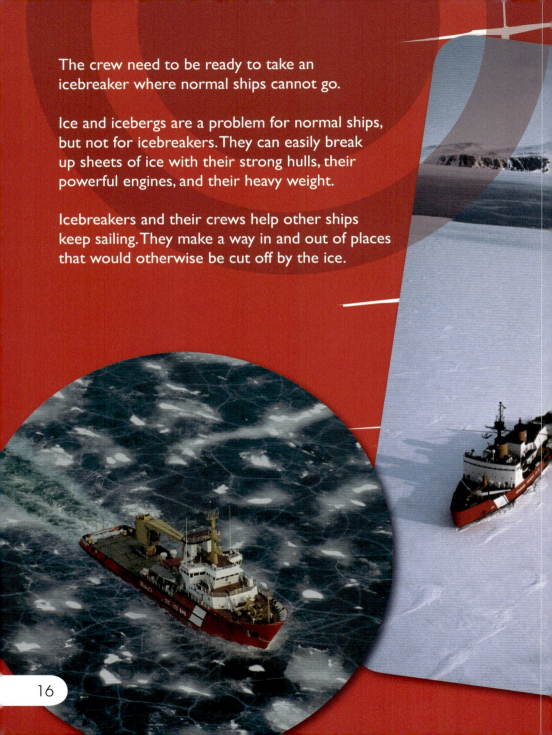

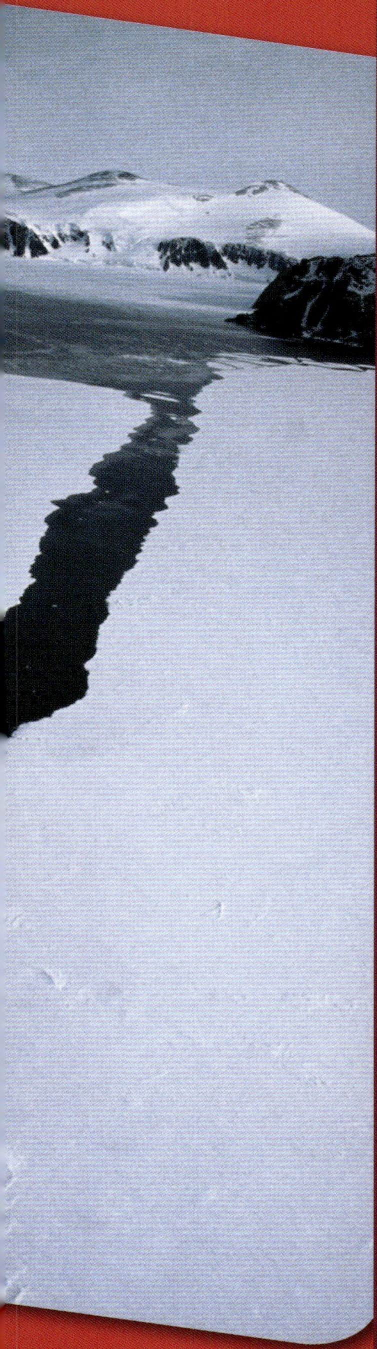

Index

Reports

How to write a report:

Reports record information.

Step One

- Choose a topic.
- Make a list of the things you know about the topic.
- Write down the things you need to find out.

Topic:
Icebreakers

What I know:

- Icebreakers are ships that break ice.
- Icebreakers clear frozen water for other ships and boats.
- Icebreakers work in cold places.

Research:
I need to find out:

- Why we have icebreakers.
- What icebreakers look like.
- What icebreakers do.
- Who works on icebreakers.

Step Two

- Research the things you need to know.
- You can go to the library, use the Internet, or ask an expert.
- Make notes.

Step Three

- Organize the information.
- Make some headings.

Why do we have icebreakers?

- to clear icy seas
- to clear ice in rivers
- to clear wharves and harbors
- to help get supplies through
- to help scientists
- to help in emergencies
- to help clean up pollution
- to warn about icebergs
- to move icebergs

The ship

- wide
- heavy
- thick hull
- hull like a knife
- huge propellers
- powerful engines

Step Four

Use your notes to write your report. You can use:

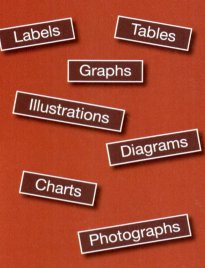

Labels

Tables

Graphs

Illustrations

Diagrams

Charts

Photographs

Your report could have...

...a contents page

Contents

...an index

Index

Some reports also have a glossary to explain difficult words.

19

Guide Notes

Title: Icebreakers

Stage: Fluency (4)

Text Form: Informational Report

Approach: Guided Reading

Processes: Thinking Critically, Exploring Language, Processing Information

Written and Visual Focus: Contents Page, Captions, Labels, Bullet Points, Flow Diagram, Index

THINKING CRITICALLY

(sample questions)

Before Reading – Establishing Prior Knowledge

- What do you know about ships that can break through ice?

Visualizing the Text Content

- What might you expect to see in this book?
- What form of writing do you think will be used by the author?
- Look at the contents page and index. Encourage the students to think about the information and make predictions about the text content.

After Reading – Interpreting the Text

- Look at pages 2 and 3. Why do you think it is important for ships to be able to move through the water all year around?
- Look at pages 4 and 5. Why do you think an icebreaker would have to pull an iceberg through the water?
- Look at pages 8 and 9. Do you think the icebreaker is a powerful ship? Why do you think that?
- Look at pages 10 and 11. Do you think the icebreaker could cut through ice that was thicker than seven feet? Why do you think that?
- Look at pages 12 and 13. What do you think might happen if the icebreaker's engines stopped?
- Look at pages 14 and 15. Why do you think there are so many crew members aboard an icebreaker?
- What do you know about icebreakers that you didn't know before?
- What in the book helped you understand the information?
- What questions do you have after reading the text?

EXPLORING LANGUAGE

Terminology

Photography credits, index, contents page, imprint information, ISBN number